pangaea

PROSE AND POETRY

HINNAH MIAN

central
avenue
PUBLISHING

2022

Content Warning:
This book contains sensitive material related to sexual assault, domestic violence, racism, mental health and other potentially upsetting topics.

Some of these pieces are based on true stories, and some may be changed to fit a different theme. No actual names are used in this collection.

Published by Central Avenue Publishing, an imprint of Central Avenue Marketing Ltd.
centralavenuepublishing.com
@centavepub

PANGAEA

Trade Paperback: 978-1-77168-258-9
Ebook: 978-1-77168-259-6

Published in Canada
Printed in United States of America

1. POETRY / Asian American 2. POETRY / Women Authors

10 9 8 7 6 5 4 3 2 1

CONTENTS

pan

learning to become

("all, entire, whole")

gaia

looking for

("mother earth, land")

To my family,
who taught me home is not a place
but the love you create there.

I EXPLODE IN QUIET

I was eleven years old when someone first called me a terrorist.

It was a blond-haired, blue-eyed boy—
the kind I was told my whole life
to be attracted to
afraid of
smaller than.

Maybe that's why I
laughed in person,
cried in private—
I had to be anything
but loud because

bombs walk around
in brown skin,
haven't you heard?

The towers fell
when I was a child
but even then, my skin
was just warm enough
to scare them.

Hurt quietly,
my mother told me,
it's safer that way.

I guess in a way,
bottling up
is a form of exploding,
and we all carry it
inside of us, quietly,
shamefully,

waiting to figure out
if this is a trigger or a heart
or something that needs to
claw out of our throats—

I am not an explosive;
I am a spark, learning
how to dim itself in a world
that keeps adding fuel to the fire.

WELCOME TO MY BODY: A WAR MEMORIAL

underneath this skin,
i have fought the battles of
me, my parents, grandparents,
a country that i have only lived in
in memories.

here, under the flesh
of my heart, a man's
corpse has settled,
decaying until it is
one with my body's system.

i am still learning how
to give a killer
a proper burial.

here, on my tongue,
i have tasted all
walks of life, but i have
still not learned how to properly
introduce myself.

i am still learning
how to decorate a
graveyard to make it
welcoming.

read the scars on
my body like braille,
for i no longer know how
to tell a story that belongs
deeply to me but is
no longer just mine.

THERE ARE MORE GUNS IN AMERICA THAN PEOPLE

Terrorist begins and ends with   tongue   on the roof of your mouth
 you have a habit of miscounting the teeth inside of you
  the ones with cavities count   don't you know
 I stared down the barrel of a gun   once   while the man
spat *terrorist* at me   me   a college student   armed with nothing
but the hair on my arms   and me   a gaping mouth
waiting to swallow   the words fed to me   by the hands
  of a whole country   bullets jingle in my mouth
like loose teeth and all I want to know at this point is
how to be effectively   lost   in a world
      not looking for me   never looking for me

FOR THOSE WHO DID NOT MAKE IT TO EID,

There is no poetic way to describe a bomb,
because a bomb does not want to be poetic.

It wants to be
the bearer of
165 lost prayers
in Baghdad.

It wants to be
what fills
the fasting bodies
right before they
pick up a date.

It wants the air
to hold the aftermath
the way stomach
holds hunger,

the way mothers
foster deaf prayers.

Bombs are not poetic,
because words can't
mesh corpses back
together.

Bombs are not poetic,
because sorrow will now

drown cities the way
earth fills
the mouths
of bodies.

Bombs are not poetic,
because they fall on
God the way pleading
knees fall on prayer-mat
remains of the dead.

PALM READINGS

Why do we hold our hands up as a form of protection against things
that we know can shatter us? A bullet, glass, car crash—all things that
are   starving   for skin, and our palms, ripe with hope and blood,
desperately pleading   a last wave   goodbye.

A man enters the room   with an assault rifle, and we hold our
hands up, as if   something as delicate as a finger
can catch something as   hungry   as a bullet.

Maybe this is a testament to the human will—
in our last moments,
pleading, forgiving, praying:
all things palms have grown
accustomed to

DIFFERENT IS SOMETIMES SYNONYMOUS WITH LONELY

When I was a kid, my brownness was alien. Girls at school would ask me why my arms were so hairy. *That's just how people look where I'm from*, I'd say. They would ask if I was maybe too dirty. Maybe I should shower more often, and then the brownness would seep into the drain like diluted tea. At home I'd scrub and scrub my skin raw, but I never saw the white underneath. Maybe the white was bone. Maybe I just needed to keep digging like a dog until I found it. Where I'm from, stray dogs did this a lot. *Kutta*. Maybe I was one of them. Girls at school would ask me if my *mehndi* was a skin condition. *No, that's just what we do where I'm from*. Suddenly, Eid was a hospital I was trying to avoid. My mom would ask why I wouldn't want the pretty patterns on the palms of my hands. I told her it looked like a rash and I couldn't afford to get any more contaminated, not when I wore my skin like a warning sign. Now my hands were plain and boring and almost beautiful. When I was a kid, brownness was sitting on the corner of the playground, wondering maybe if I just sat still enough, I'd get confused with the earth and I wouldn't be seen. I would just be all things soil and flourishing because this planet looked like me and it was *where I'm from* and I didn't know why I was the only one who could see it.

IN THE INTEREST OF NOT GETTING TOO
POLITICAL, LET ME JUST SAY THIS:

There is nothing political about the way
a body breaks.

The body cares not for what
is right or left or in front of our eyes.
It only knows how to do what a body does:

carry on in spite of it all.

When the bomb swallows
my countrymen whole,
we do not think about
the politics of it.

They explode the way
bodies do: not remembering
the human form, only remembering
what it means to be
beautifully horrific and finite.

America, my people
don't care for your politics,
because there is nothing
political about humanity—

we were born without borders
until your politics put them there,
creating confines for
our brown bodies to break between.

FOR THE MAN WHO COLONIZED MY BODY

my mother tells me of how
her homeland was once
taken over by those who
felt as though they
were entitled to it
simply because she
wasn't pretty enough
to call it her own

i can't tell if it's my
memory or hers
when i see the
stare of a soldier
holding his gun as
if its bullets
belonged in my body
as much as i
was supposed to belong
on this soil

she tells me we are
blessed to have a home
on both ends of the world
and i tell her it is a curse
to not belong to
either of them

my mother tells me of how
disappointed she was in me

when i had my land
taken over by
a man who felt as though
he was entitled to it
simply because i was too
pretty to not share it

he left his marks on me
the way the bombs
left their marks on
my mother's hometown
when she was learning
how to be a little girl
in the comfort of her
own bomb shelter

she tells me of how
she was taught to
avoid the men marching
around with big guns
and uniforms because
they always had a hand on
the trigger

i tell her it is
hard to avoid them
when nowadays
everyone seems to
conceal their weapons

my mother tells me
the biggest regret

she ever had
was to let her country
get taken over by
those who don't even
recognize
its beauty

she doesn't seem
to realize it
hurts the same
even as they
whisper "you're
so beautiful"
as they are
conquering
your body

HANDLING HOUSE FIRES

how much darkness   is enough darkness
for us to finally   see the light again
we can't keep burning down villages
for   temporary warmth   we can't keep
swallowing bullets   because we neglected
hunger   it has been nighttime for far too
long   can't you see that the stars are not stars
but rips in our fabric   they just want
to see the sun again   who do you pray to
when the god who has blessed
this land watches as
we bury ourselves alive   saying
it matters not as long   as the flowers
we spit up   sit pretty on our graves

THE LANGUAGE OF PROMISES

When I was a kid my mom would force me to read the Quran start to finish, but she never bothered to teach me the language—I always thought, *How can this be prayer if I don't know what I'm praying for?* And maybe this is why I make empty promises but murmur them in a voice that calms you enough to believe me. Read my body like the scripture it is, and let's pray for a future neither of us believes in. At least it will sound lovely for the night. I'm sorry I don't know how to be holy enough to learn the language of the promises I'm making.

THERE IS NOTHING ELEGANT ABOUT THE WAY A KINGDOM BURNS

I know what it means to be wanted and unwanted—
    America, to be home in you is to
    throw away a first skin.

I am beautiful only when my legs are open
    and I have forgotten my mother tongue
    to make room for yours.

i.

There is nothing elegant about the way a kingdom burns. It is easy
not to get burnt when sitting on a throne.

i.

I know I'm American, because death is an old friend you see at the
grocery stores, the movies, church—a familiar haunting that we have
learned to live with.

i.

I've never fucked a brown girl before, whispered to me like it's my name.
Exotic drips from his tongue like liquor, and now I wonder if I am a
body or a person or neither.

    I am left like tea leaves—used up,
    what sweetness lives within me fucked dry,
    disposed of when I no longer have worth.

To be brown and woman here is to be bodiless. To belong to something that does not resemble yourself.

They say you can read tea leaves at the bottom of your cup, and my sprawled limbs read *I should thank you for tasting me*.

I didn't want to. But I did.

HOME / SICKNESS

They always tell me that I'll be okay when I tell them how
much I belong deeply to anywhere but here

They don't know what it's like to
live in a house that wants nothing
more than to collapse, to live
every day in fear of a failing foundation

How do I place trust
in a system that was
built with the intention
of breaking?

THE FIRST TIME I WAS TOLD TO WATCH SOMETHING DIE

I was a young girl,
as small as the lamb
the axe beheaded—

I remember only turning away
and the pools of blood underneath our feet.

Since then, watching something die
has become as commonplace as
the ads on TV—

as an American, death has become
as patriotic as the blood-red flags
that we are taught to respect more than
human bodies.

Every time I step outside,
I feel like the lamb,
waiting for the axe,
waiting for my turn
to serve my country.

LAHORE BLAST

The world does not cry for us.

They watch a mother
fall to her knees
as if at prayer,
kneeling before the body of her baby,
her forehead resting on the corpse
as if she is performing *sajdah*.

The world will not cry for us.

They are white church halls,
white church dresses,
white hands coming together
to form a prayer not meant
for the dirt road–colored skin
of my people,
white hands refusing to pick up
the remains of 72 brown bodies—
we lie in the mud
and you call it camouflage
and step over us.

The world is not crying for us.

They do not know
that our skin is not mud,
it is the spiciness of chai and
the sweetness of halwa.

They do not know
that this playground is not
a battleground,
these little bodies
are not soldiers—

You wail for God,
but when we do the same,
you say the bomb blast
deafened your ears
so you did not hear us.

A BETTER LIFE

what my mother did not
teach me as a kid
was how to feel when
looking into the barrel
of a gun.

my mother taught me
how to appreciate life
on this side of the world,
having left her home
and everything she loved
to give her children
"a better life."

my mother now
chokes back tears
when trying to get
the words "a better life"
to crawl out of her throat.

what my mother
did not teach me
as a kid was to
handle the fear
of living my life.

my mother always
told me pretty white lies
to try and ease the pain

of the future and because of that,
i had to teach myself
how to be a kid,
but i also had to teach myself
how to save the life of one.

i first got a gun pulled on me
at age 18 because my skin
did not match the color
of the stars and stripes.

my mother was not surprised
when i told her. instead she
dreamily reminisced about her
childhood in her home country,
a time when she and the world
felt safe.

what my school
did not teach me
as a kid
was that all these
foreign countries are
not war torn, dangerous,
pillaged of hope.
that my home is not
a battlefield.

they were trying to
distract me from the
fact that i am
currently living on one.

I AM NO LONGER IN THE BUSINESS OF TURNING RAGE INTO SILENCE

This country collects too many tongues, until our only language becomes quiet. This is me screaming. I am no longer watering myself down just so I don't get caught in your throat. Our rage is too bright for you to dim down. We are tired of being exit wounds.

BACKPACKS AND BOMBINGS

We're gathered around the kitchen table.
Between laughter, my father
tells us a story
about how, when he was a kid
on his way home from school,
the bombs would drop.
And, as if shielding heads from the rain,
he and his friend would run home,
backpacks over the head
like an umbrella for warfare.

On the TV in the living room,
another school shooting is announced.
This time, they suggest the solution
would be to market bulletproof backpacks.
As if children, like a mother,
only know how to hold false protection
in their arms.

I often think about how I—
a daughter of immigrants—
was born into a life
so foreign to that
of her parents.
But maybe we're not so
different
after all.

WHO I'M ALLOWED TO BE

I don't know how much of me / I'm allowed to be / on this side of the sea / I have to water myself down like tea / some days I'm scared to go outside / and others I want to scream / *here i am* / my mother tells me not to be myself too loudly / because lately people like me have become explosives / she also tells me that she is proud of me / for being brave but I'm not brave / I'm just numb / watered down / trying to learn who I am / and who I'm allowed to be

HAIR LIKE THE SUN

I once wore long-sleeve shirts every day of the year for seven years to hide the long, dark hair on my arms.

When I was in elementary school, I made the mistake of skipping a day and a little girl, hair like the sun, told me I looked like an animal.

I came home crying, begging for the bleaching cream my mother usually saved for my face, and asked why I couldn't use it everywhere.

I realized what I was really asking was why I couldn't have been born with hair like the sun, skin white, hair soft enough to be overlooked.

No matter how much I wear to cover my skin, I can never seem to hide it enough.

MY COUNTRY WAS THE FIRST TO FUCK ME

She held me close when she did so. Promised me things I was fooled
into thinking I'd receive. She ran her lips all over me. Told me I was
beautiful but not worth the time. Her words were so pretty. I wore
them like makeup. Armor. Lighter skin. The kind that would glow
softly in a room.

She held me that night like I was a momentary comfort. A thing to be
used. I'd be tossed out when morning came.

And there I found myself, sun-soaked on a sidewalk, tripping
desperately for a home I knew I'd never find.

They could see her tangled in my hair as I stumbled back. Could
smell her skin still perfumed on me. Maybe that's why they were too
scared to talk to me. I was another one of her rejects. An afterthought.
A morning after.

Can you help me? I'm lost.

They stayed silent. They always do.

I do not belong to me. Here. A place that   birthed me   left me
kissed me   but
hated the taste.

LEARNING TO LOVE BOMB-THREAT BODIES

I.

Brown bodies often get confused
with mines nowadays, and
when you told me you were
scared you'd get caught in
the explosion, I didn't
blame you.

This heart resembles
a grenade, and when it
bounced off the
walls in my chest
as we moved like
heat waves on the
bed, I think we both
feared for our lives.

II.

I always felt dangerous
in my skin, and when you
told me you found the color
of it to look more like cinnamon
than mud, you decided that
our shades of dangerous would
look even more beautiful
together.

We taped our
gunpowdered torsos
shut with each other's
skin so that if we were
to go out in flames—
at least we'd destruct
together.

III.

I've learned that
my body is a prayer
and not an explosion.

IV.

You treated it
like a bomb threat—
handled it tentatively,
tiptoed around me
as if you wanted
to set me off
because you
mistakenly thought
that self-destruction
was a hue of
beautiful
rather than
a hue of
tragic.

V.

You should've
held my name
in your mouth
like a prayer.

Not a bomb threat.

You should've
treated my body
as if you were
tasting a slice
of divinity,
not treading
across a minefield.

VI.

This brown body is
not an explosion;
it is light and honey—
all things heaven
wants to
die into.

HENNA

a girl with skin like autumn,
used to the transition,
the fleeting, the vibrant and fading
skin like *mehndi*, transient,
used for its beauty
and temporary touch—
for once, i want to be something that lasts.

ON BEING A BANDAGE

I remember holding a bomb in comfort as it exploded
        I don't know why women   are born into the role of
bandages   I never wanted to soak
up all your blood   it just happened that way
        I doubt my mother ever expected
to give birth to explosives   *sorry mother   I wanted to shine*
        bright but not   this bright
I don't know how to be a womb   I only know how to
foster dead things   in their last moments
I won't apologize for taking care of you   I only
wish I knew how to exist properly in the process

ON NOT KNOWING HOW TO BELIEVE IN GOD

Do you know what it is like to hold your name in my mouth, when
my parents have always thought that I only hold God's? When
they were my age, if they had found prayers hidden between lies
and rendezvous like we did, they would have had their forgiveness
burned into them. Instead, I burned your love into my skin.

I carry shame like a souvenir of our escapades, but we often prayed
together, anyway. You thank me for helping you find your identity
before you say goodbye to me forever. My mother curses you for
taking away hers when you took away my innocence.

I have always filled the space between my thighs with divinity, and I
often confused your moans for prayers. I still do. I couldn't recite you
a single *surat* of the Quran but if you asked me what your order was
from your favorite restaurant, I'd repeat it in a heartbeat.

Dear God, I'm so sorry that we loved until we damned each other.

AN APOLOGY

I am so disappointed in you, my mother says to me
after she learns that I let a man
hurt me.

She tells me of when large men
with guns colonized her land
as she stood by and watched
her home crumble into
an aftermath.

I tell her how lies
can sound as pretty as
a promise,
how gunshots
can sound like
fireworks,
how *I didn't mean to hurt you*
can sound like
I didn't mean to fall in love with you.

She tells me how she
was forced to live
in the comfort of her
own bomb shelter

and how it is a
disgrace that I
willingly armed
the man who
colonized my body.

I say that I am sorry,
but I can no longer tell
which of us
I am saying it to.

CONFESSIONS TO MY MOTHER

I was always afraid
to tell my mother
that a man
loved me.

I was always afraid
that she'd think
my body was no
longer a home
to divinity—

that the *zamzam*
in my veins
was now tainted
with his touch.

I was always afraid
that she would know
we shared a bed,
a soul,
a home—

that her little girl
had been tasted
by a man.

I was always afraid
to tell my mother
that a man
broke me.

I was afraid
that she'd think
her little girl's
body was the site
of a losing battle.

I was afraid
that she'd think
I gave up
my body—a temple,
a holy scripture—
to one who could not
feel the divinity
inside it.

When I told her
these things
she looked at me,
put a trembling hand
on my cheek
and said,

"*Pari,*
a man who
truly loves you
will never break you.

Not everyone
who has the
honor of speaking
a prayer believes
in the words
rolling off
their tongue."

THE COMPOSITION OF BONES

You say that I am magic
though I am but clay
and crushed leaves
held together with
the honey of my
mother's chai,

I am but the remains
of a person left
crawling
out of the ashes,
crawling
until my elbows
bleed light, until the
cuts and bruises on my
brown skin scream,
"میں زندہ ہوں
میں زندہ ہوں
میں زندہ ہوں
I am alive!"

My sweet,
my bones are not made up of magic

but of the tubes leading
into my grandmother's
lungs,

of the drops of blood left

by my lover's hands
that I had to wipe
with the fabric
of my own clothes.

It is the composition
of the deaf
surats that fell
with an explosion
from my mother's lips
and onto the homes
of my countrymen.

My sweet,
I wish I were as easy as magic,

but I am as mute as prayer,
as broken as promise,
as powerful as hope.

Love me like I am
the last words you will
whisper to God—

not a spell,
but a knowing.

Not a spell,
but a blessing.

LETTER TO MY MOTHER'S WEDDING PHOTO

This is a letter to the girl in a sepia photo,
head dressed in ornate hand-beaded scarves,
hands embroidered with earth-hued henna.
She is years younger than I am now
but has lived lifetimes of stories and poems
I could only dream of,
living in a country I only
call home in passed-down memories.
Mother, I am so sorry I could not be that girl too.
I am so sorry America has turned me into a stranger,
both in mirrors and photographs.
You named me after the henna that kissed
your nimble hands the way I should have,
and I'm sorry that the only part of the henna I inherited is the fading
and not the beauty.
Your wedding gown—intricate and golden—was never
done justice in the faded hue of the photo.
It's okay though—that is how I'll always remember you:
beautiful and golden and everything I can never be.

HOLY LANDS

If you wish
to read the story
of my people,
look no further
than my body.

My silhouette, an ocean.
Your lips, a sailor.

Every beauty mark, a country to roam.
Every stretch mark, a river to cross.

Explore the lands
you were always told
were forbidden.
Find home in a
space that was
never meant
to be yours.

Make your way
down to the village
of my hips.
Seek refuge in the space
between my bones.

Become familiar
with the apparatus
of your new holy land,

for you will try to
tell yourself you
cannot stay, but never
gather the strength
to leave.

A PREFACE TO MY THOUGHTS

I want to be more than myself / some days I feel so small / what am I but a bird's-eye view / of a possibility / I breathe in lungfuls of tomorrow / but all I exhale is yesterday / what I mean is / I waited for you my whole life / and you were taken away / just as quick as you came / what I'm saying is / I feel so lost here / in my home / I belong deeply to memories of elsewhere / you were there often / but I know better than to / build houses in people now / it is so easy to relapse into sorrow / when you were forged from it / I don't know what I belong to / whether it is to the universe / my homeland / or an empty promise / I am just tired / of scattering pieces of my body / everywhere but here

PANGAEA

My parents loved without borders—
a love that knew no continents,
a love buoyant enough to never
sink on any sea.

My parents held hands across time—
fingers like nomads, ever-exploring,
jagged edges of border walls nothing but
a test to prove how rugged their
hands had grown from breaking
down barriers.

My parents cut around fault lines,
creating edges that would
only fit perfectly with the other—
all to prove that there was
never any fault in their love
at all.

My love,
if oceans scare you,
remember my body
is made up of
the blood of maps.

I am a child of borderlines
and we are two lands,
carved differently.

Love is the way
we conquer:
boundaries, lands,
time, distance,
history.

It is the way
we were built.

IF THERE'S ONE THING I'VE LEARNED, IT'S THAT PRAYER IS NOT TRANSACTIONAL

if anything, it is a shift of power,
a begging, an abusive relationship.

how many times must we pray for change
before blood stops pouring?

why are we taught to fear God more than
we are to love him? if he were not
portrayed as a man, would it be the same way?

I guess what I'm trying to say is
I was taught to love you
the same way I was taught to worship:

all-consuming, fear first,
knees and head on the floor,
begging for you to accept me.

LOVING YOU LIKE MY HOMELAND

I talk of you the way
I remember my country—
a place I call my home
even though I am hardly
ever there.

A land I remember
in vague, beautiful
images, like I am
looking at our old pictures
through misty eyes.

Your name sounds
like my native tongue—
something I understand
perfectly but can hardly speak
because I was never taught
how to hold the words
properly in my mouth.

Your hello echoes
in my memory
like a call to prayer
cutting through the air,
a reminder not to forget
the divine love
that revived you.

I loved you

like I barely
had a land
to call my own,
a body born between
two worlds; I can't help
that I am constantly
feeling lost—
when you left,
it was nothing new,
but left me feeling homesick
all the same.

THE FUNNY THING ABOUT TRAUMA IS

you don't know it's there
until it's long gone.
That's how you exist—

in the aftermath, the reminiscence,
a thorn stuck in the past tense.

When memories are no longer
memories but flashbacks,
that is when I know
you run deeper
than any wound.

When they tell me
to just get over it,
I tell them
I am not equipped
to dig that deep
inside the human body.

They don't understand
you're not a surface wound
but a tumor growing
and darkening with time.

ON TRANSLATING HIM

I crave the broken love he makes to me.

The way he conveys in a lost language
of silences and curled fists
that God created this
misfit love to remind us
how oftentimes, damaged things
are to be left damaged.

I have so often tried to
learn this language
just so I could talk to him
that I forget my native
tongue entirely.

It's so hard
to choke out the
words "I love you"
when he gets the
world to curl its
fingers around
my throat.

The way he
tells me I am his—
I don't seem to mind
if it's with his lips
or his absence.

He promises me they
mean the same thing.

Learning a language
takes a while,
I tell myself.

He loves like
food to the hungry,
like blankets to
the freezing,
like prayers
to the lost,
like salt
to the wounded.

I don't care that
I've given
myself entirely
to his breathing—

whether it be
in her ear
or mine.

We're both just learning his language.

LOVE IS BLIND

I tell myself that the bruises on your knuckles
are just galaxies that I am blessed to look at.

I tell myself that it is okay that
I can see the veins
branching on your neck
when you are screaming at me
—I hope to see flowers blossom on them one day.

I tell myself that it is okay
that you stumble into our room
intoxicated at three in the morning,
because the words "I love you"
are just as beautiful
slurred.

I tell myself that it is okay
to feel so hurt,
because your kisses
are so sweet that I can no longer
taste the bitter.

On your worst days,
I still find sonnets in your half-smiles.

I GUESS IT'S MY FAULT FOR OPENING THE DOOR

I've been over the locks on my heart a hundred times—polished the chains until they were silver enough to see my own reflection. This is how healing goes sometimes. In halfway points: loving in halves. Handling in halves. Opening up again in halves. It is hard to do things wholly when you have once been shattered.

I didn't open halfway, though.
You knocked.

And I broke open like a dam. Poured myself into the first warm thing my body felt after years of darkness.

What else is the heart but a fist pounding on a door, over and over, a door that leads nowhere? I am so tired of knocking on the entrance to a purgatory.

Too often, I am the waiting room and not the destination.

Dust your feet on the welcome mat before entering me.
I have a habit of not washing away footprints.

LOVING AGAIN IN THE AFTERMATH

My last lover had hands that broke me.

I'm sorry, he still lives within me sometimes.

But I still want to love you. I do. I'm sorry if his voice is still screaming inside me when I open my mouth. A haunting echo reverberating in my lungs. Don't listen. Don't listen. I don't want to either.

You are so beautiful, but I'm sorry if sometimes I don't know whether it's a mask or not. I saw a man rip his skin off right in front of me once. And now sometimes when I run my hands over you, I look for corners that lift. It's just a habit.

I want to love you wholly. I will one day. Please be patient with me.

ON DROWNING

You look for me every time you stand at the mouth of the sea.

I often let myself drown just to remind myself how lovely it was to breathe. Don't come searching for me; I know not where I am. I only know that I spell your name constantly, rearranging seashells so they will be even more beautiful when they form the curves of it. It is all that I know—like a siren's call: how alluring it sounds—and yet it wants nothing more than to grasp you by the throat and pull you under.

This suffocation is a blanket and I yearn only to lie under it. If loving you is asphyxiation, then I will pick up a shell and carve gills into my neck.

I KEEP REMEMBERING NEW THINGS

In the film of smoke I see our ghosts, dancing,
tethered to our past bodies.

Another average Tuesday night: heavy, like tar. You
told me to pack my things and go.
And yelled at me when I picked up my bag.

I blow out the smoke and our silhouette dissipates, like spit on water.

It is fascinating how
the night can be so many
things at once—a memory
and a discovery and a coping
mechanism—which is to say,
I can't remember the last time
the sun came up.

You were probably there.

Thanking me for dragging it
up and consequently burning
just bright enough to light
your path.

I'LL BE WRITING ABOUT YOU FOREVER

I think I so often write about you because that is the last time my heart remembers feeling anything at all—which begs the question, what, exactly, did you do to me to be able to revive a dead thing so easily?

I honestly miss the heartbreak because at least it allows me to reassure myself that I am still human—alive, feeling.

Isn't the real tragedy not mourning the loss of you, but mourning loss?

I would welcome in the heartbreak with a familiarity I haven't experienced in years. I guess that means I'll be writing about you forever.

THIS DYSLEXIC LOVE

I know I often
stumble over
words when you
talk to me,

but how could
I possibly confuse
you writing *In the morning,*
I will be gone
all over my body,
with your lips
parting on my bare skin
with *I love you.*

This dyslexic love
has me rearranging
the letters of *Lie to me*
to *Love me,*
and for a second
I confuse your pulse
for mine and it sounds
a lot like my sighs,

and I am so
distracted by your
breath perfuming
my neck that I don't
hear you whispering
that I'm a fool
in my ears

and your tongue
writing *Goodbye*
in my mouth
tastes like heaven

and I curse
myself for claiming
that I am a
creator of words
when I can't even read
the red flags
that you're
scratching on my back.

GASLIGHTINGS AND EXORCISMS

Tell me how a person can inhabit you
and make you forget yourself
entirely.

How you can breathe them
in like smoke and become
more sky than person.
I know the sky is blue.
You keep telling me it's black
and it's all I see now.

Tell me how a person can
sneak inside you and paint
the insides of your lids
whatever picture they see.
You tell me I should be
thankful for the art.

I know the words to recite
when practicing an exorcism,
but you've already grabbed
ahold of my tongue and I'm
too busy moaning to mind.

THE ANATOMY OF HAUNTING

I am so
        tired
of harboring
your ghost
in me.

I am so
        tired
of loving like
a wounded home
too worn and
too inhabited by
old memories
to make room
for newcomers.

You were always
the superstitious
type, and I always
laughed at you when
you'd tell me that you
would never live in
a house, because houses
were too easy to haunt.

I never took you seriously until now.

You made a
house out of me,

and now your
touch still lingers
between every single
one of my fingers.

Why couldn't I
see that I was
inhaling you,
giving you
permission
to possess me
when our lips touched?

Welcome home.

I didn't know
that you were
wearing me down so
you could inhabit the
cracks in my bones,
slipping into the fractures
like a mist until you
encompassed me from the
inside out.

I didn't know
that you were
making a crawl space
out of my rib cage
so I could always feel
you there —
            somewhere.

Somewhere in these
walls, our ghosts
are still slow-dancing
in my stomach,
and with every step,
I can feel it
drop further
and further
              down.

The anatomy of
this haunting
has me tearing
myself apart
limb
          from
                      limb
just so I can
finally
get a chance
to see you again.

I GUESS THIS IS ME BEING VULNERABLE:

I haven't felt anything in   months. I forget what it means to have
skin.

I forget what it means to be hungry.   My skin   aches. For you, I
will

let   myself   yearn   again. Bare again. Bear again.   This is how I
look when I am

naked.   Without skin.   Organs first.   Every beat of the heart
resting—

not resting—on an overturned wrist.   I admit, it has been a
minute.   I've

fucked a lot of people, but I haven't slept next to anyone in a while. I
like the way

you dream against my skin.   You jerk in your sleep, you know?
It's

okay.   It makes your heart beat heavy against my back.   It's the
most human

thing I've felt in   years.   I've been more absence than person. I
am

composed more of   the empty space   between bones than I am
blood.

What I mean is,   all I ever do is write about someone. Lately, I've
been writing *to*

someone.   I know it's hard to listen.   Lately, I can hear again. Here
again.

Falling hard again. I don't know how   to be present   in an   absent
body.

But I want to be. For the first time   in a long time. I hope that's okay
with

you.

I WROTE A BOOK ABOUT BECOMING WHOLE AND TONIGHT, I'M THE LAST BOTTLE OF ALCOHOL IN THE FRIDGE

In another language my
name means "between,"
and it all makes so much
sense that I was born to be
lost in the border of worlds.

Tonight, I am the in-between
of healing and collapsing,
and I understand the way foundations feel
when the Earth grabs ahold of them
just to have them tremble in its palms—
Here is a reminder
of who you belong to.

Tonight, I am the in-between
of home and homeless,
remembering a land taken from me
before I was born, a place where
I would never have written
this poem but perhaps
could have written an
entirely different story.

And tonight, I am the in-between
distance of you and me—
a big, gaping hole—
and I keep throwing myself in,

hoping I'll eventually
fill the stretch   but I don't know how
to be a bridge   I only know
how to be the   empty space   between us.

STOP LOOKING FOR THINGS TO GO WRONG

your love tastes
like the first sip
of morning coffee—
a wake-up
call, a burning,
an encompassing
warmth—
something I must
take advantage of
before
it gets cold.

HOW TO BE LOVED BY HIM

Accept that I call you beautiful, but also accept what I tell you is not.

Accept that you are not allowed to be brighter than me—exist solely in my shadow, which only disappears when I turn around to look at you.

Accept that my promises are just words that I like to throw around like knives. But believe in them anyway, the way you want to believe in me.

Accept that you are only allowed to be in my life when I feel as though I am ready to love you. Otherwise, I'll make you feel unwanted.

Accept that I was conditioned to feel broken, so that when I try to rebuild myself, I will blame you for every single thing I get wrong so that I still feel like I am growing.

Accept that I learned love from my mother, so I think it is the way someone runs back to you after you hurt them and hurt them.

Accept that I learned absence from my father, so I will beg and beg you to stay but push you away so that I can ready myself for the disappearance.

Accept that I will love you so deeply and passionately that when I abuse you, you will excuse it because you yearn for me the way an addict yearns for their fix.

Accept that I am a drug—I will destroy you from the inside out but make you feel euphoric while doing so.

THE UNIVERSE IS TELLING ME I'M GREAT, BUT MY DEPRESSION IS TELLING ME OTHERWISE

i keep trying to inhale
parts of the universe
in order to feel whole
in my stomach   maybe if i
stitch myself into   galaxies then
i will be as vivid   as i feel
i don't know how to
scream into a soundless void
that i am brilliant   bright   beautiful
all i know is how
to feel it in the pit of my gut

even the sun learns to love
its burning, learns to love
the carry of its burdening
too often   i tend to
wear the universe   like a bruise
and call it becoming
i need to learn how to carry
my own body the way a galaxy
carries its possibilities—
carefully   endlessly   proudly
the way a planet   learns to create

HOW DO YOU LOVE A DEAD GIRL?

I remember when the first man I loved told me that I was too sad to love—that the dark cloud inside me was louder than my love for him.

The second man I loved told me he didn't know how to love a depressed woman.

I don't know how to be stronger than my storms.

Some days I am more complete than others.

Some days I wonder if I'll ever be whole at all.

How do you warn someone not to love you?

I am a virus, I want to say. I'm a selfish lover.

Run far away. But take me with you.

How do you love a dead girl?

I'm still learning, my love. I'm still learning.

EXPLAINING MY DEPRESSION TO MY LOVER

i am tired
but not that kind of tired
not the sleep kind of tired

the kind of tired that lives
in your bones and weighs
more than your body

the kind that settles
under your eyes like
a gray cloud over a village

what i mean by *i am tired* is
i'm so sorry please don't hate me

what i mean by *i am tired* is
i really want to love you better

what i mean by *i am tired* is
i didn't mean to bleed out
when i cut you from my veins

what i mean is
some nights i am less star
and more the darkness that shrouds them

what i mean is
i am so sorry
but last night i relapsed again
and it tasted like you

and in the heat of my own undoing
i burnt down our home
and spelled your name in the ashes

i'm sorry i just
don't know what
else to say

and when you say
is it me?

all i can say is no,
no. when i say i'm tired
what i really mean is
i am a hostage
to myself.

PROZAC HAS NUMBED ME TO GRIEF

so instead i let the world fall apart
around me and watch my potential
crumble like cities burning to
the ground. i let ashes fall
like darkened winter
and hope that one day
i can find enough parts of me
in the rubble to rebuild
all that i used to be

DEPRESSION WAVES

I am tired of living
inside myself,

each blink a
collapsing morning.

It is beautiful
watching stars die,
no matter how dull the star.

We all fear falling—

the star's last burden
to carry a wish,

a life's last burden
to do nothing but cast them.

A READING OF MY BODY

i will be blunt:

there is no part of me that
will ever be able
to forget you.

i am sorry
my body is not
a clean slate.

i collect poems on my skin.

your body is
scrawled
all over me.

i've been too tired
to wash it away—
maybe i don't know
how to.

i like to trace the ghosts
of your fingers on
the back of my hand.

they read:
i don't know how
to hold without you.

lately, i've let
everything slip
through my fingers.

forgive my hands;

they're tired from
missing you.

HOOKUP

You wake like a morning:
> softly
> slowly
> quietly

I dare not disturb
something as fleeting
as a sunrise

The beauty so temporary,
gone as quickly as it dawns

I cannot curse what
I've always known was
a momentary bliss

ON LEARNING TO LOVE A SHIPWRECK

Our bodies
ebb and flow
on the bed
like debris littering
the storm-riddled sea.

We crash onto and into
each other as if
our bodies colliding
can mesh us into
something whole again.

The feel of your skin,
waves underneath mine,
is so soothing that I ignore
that we are only
floating like this
to forget that
in the morning
we drown.

I want to learn
to love
my driftwood body
without the feel of yours
on top of it.

I lie here,
back against the

sea of blankets,
reaching for the empty
space next to me
until my bones feel
settled without
yours beside them.

LATELY I'VE BEEN STAGNANT

Which is to say
I have been planted
by the wrong hands.

I grow eerily into an
unfamiliar world.

My limbs tangle in
the shadows of leaves,
shrouding me like
a numb lover.

I wonder what it
would be like
to have legs that
move forward so easily.

But mine are grounded,
buried waist-deep till I
am left lonely in a way
only forests could feel:

watching life grow
upward around them.

MULTITUDES

i.

Shadow: a darkness haloed by light.

A tomorrow often stalked by the knowledge
that we are just two
falling rays of sun
peeking through
the curtains of an old
hotel room.

ii.

I held you the way
light holds shadow.

iii.

You, a color yet
        to be discovered.

You, a pain the
        English language does not know.

I often wonder how
blood can taste like
honey, like morning
coffee diluted with milk,
golden and warm

and all things
       you.

       iv.

I wanted to tell you
that we didn't have
to love each other like war,

like how our ancestors
would kiss
to hide in each other's
mouths when the soldiers
would march.

We don't have to be
a passed-down memory.

We don't have to fight
just to exhale the
trauma from
an ancestral ghost.

       v.

Let us not touch each other to prove that we are still here. Let us
touch each other to forget that we are.

       vi.

We are so much more
       than skin can hold.

We are cupped hands
      collecting an overflow of water from the well.

We are the screams of
      your mother, the absence of your father.

How does one love a person
      who is not a person—but a multitude?

      vii.

I think we would often
rub each other's skin
to peel back layers
until we would finally
find each other
underneath all
the flesh.

      I told myself the bleeding
      was worth it.

I'M SORRY THAT I FIGURED YOU OUT

I'm sorry
you were
never properly
given love
and it made you
cold.

I'm sorry that
your heart is
a box painted
red with the word
FRAGILE
and you've spent
years building
cement walls
around it so
no one would ever
read it.

I'm sorry that
I've lain on
your chest so
often that I know
your body's language
well enough to hear
that word thumping
ever so softly
between your heartbeats.

I'm sorry that I figured you out.

I'm sorry that
you didn't know
how to handle
loving and being
loved so you
tried to rip it—
and me—
to shreds.

I'm sorry I let you.

A PORTRAIT AS THE FLOWERS ON A GRAVE

I am morbid,
like a garden.

What I mean by this is—
I carry around a bouquet
of bodies in my chest.

A flower for every
man who planted himself
in me, only to later
reveal himself a weed.

I don't know how to
rid myself of them
so I carry them around,

carry loss around,

like a flower:
a delicate, thriving thing
that only shortens its lifespan
when yanked like a bandage.

THE MESSAGE I'LL NEVER LEAVE YOU

I heard your voice in a video today, and it was only then that I realized I was starting to forget it.

It takes everything in me not to call you so I can remind myself, again, how beautiful it is.

I'm still dealing with your aftermath. I think I will for the rest of my life. And I want to hate you for it. Your ghost lingers in every mundane aspect of my day.

The other day, I was washing dishes, and I remembered how you used to yell at me while I was doing them because you'd confuse your mess for mine, the same way you often did with every mess in your life.

I'm scared to do dishes now.

But somehow, I remember your smile more often than the face you made when you wanted to hurt me.

I'm not drunk yet, but I just remembered that the last thing you said to me was *Yeah, I'll see you around*, and I want to cry because I know that neither of us wants to see each other even though all I want to do is lie in your arms one last time.

Remember when you used to call me just to tell me a stupid joke? I heard this joke the other day, and I want to leave it in your voice mail because I know it'd make you laugh, but I know the thought of my voice leaves a bitter taste in your mouth that you can't wash down with liquor.

Do you do that? See something and think, *She would like this*.

Yesterday, a Muslim man was beaten on his way to the mosque, and I wanted to mourn with you because no one else knows how to hold me while I cry for strangers quite the way you do, but I just remembered that you're a stranger now, and now I'm crying for the both of you.

Hello? Are you there?

I've called to remind you how my voice sounds. I hope you still hear it in the silence sometimes, the same way I hear yours.

[SORRY I'VE BEEN GHOSTING LATELY]—

i don't know how to tell you
         i've woven you into moonlight
i have a habit of losing ethereal things
         i know a part of us still lives where
the sky meets ocean, i just don't know
         how to get there anymore

i've been a little lost lately
         they say those who walk along
the water in search of something
         have a tendency to haunt
i don't want to haunt i just want to remember
         but memories tend to float like ghosts
like moonlight rippling on water

i guess a haunting
         is just a ripple
a wave passing through
         to something greater
and i am just a ghost of fingertips
         wading through water

I DON'T THINK MY FATHER REMEMBERS THIS BUT

when i was 14, he backed me
into a wall, told me that i was going
to hell for kissing a boy. i did not know
why but i knew one thing for certain:
love was not supposed to hurt like this.

not even half a decade later,
i was thrown against a wall,
sitting in fear, listening to a man
i loved tell me how unworthy
my skin was if it did not
belong to him. i didn't know
why but i knew one thing for certain:
love shouldn't have to hurt like this.

what they both had in common
was that they thought my body
was a thing to own, not a thing to love.

TRAUMA IS FOREVER

The day I learned
that trauma is forever,

that I will always have
a heavy weight
in my chest,

I was sitting on my bed
like any other day.

I heard a line on TV
that he said to me once—

And there were the memories,
crawling out of the screen,
clawing into my ears,
replaying like a continuous loop.

And then I knew
you'd always be there,
somewhere.

Goodbye never really means gone.

And every time they tell
me to get over it I want to tell them—
I have.

Just because it is over
does not mean it is dead.

[WRITER'S BLOCK]

I don't know how to write when I am not in love / when I don't have
agony seeping through my pores / I don't know where my words
go when my heart is intact / you took my tongue with you then
you walked out of my head / which is to say, where does poetry go
without a muse? / I hate you for leaving me so empty / yet giving me
more than I've ever known.

WATCHING THE FULL MOON FROM THE BALCONY

I could write about the moon and how
it rises so beautifully over our horizon,
but I'd rather write about the way
you are a silver wave dancing, drowning
me inside out. You pour out of me—
a waterfall from my eyes, mouth.
Here I am gasping for air like I am
more sea than breath   and I never thought something as beautiful as
an ocean could hurt me like this.
And yet here you are, floating,
looking down at me the way a moon does:

       glowing,   full,   staring

    so elegantly   while I drown.

FLASHBACKS

I MAKE ROOM FOR YOU IN MY HEAD
THE WAY AIR MAKES ROOM FOR A BULLET

I HAVE NO CHOICE BUT TO LET YOU LIVE HERE
HERE, AN EMPTINESS ONLY EVER DISTURBED BY AN
UNWELCOME SCAR

MY SPACE CARESSES THE AIR YOU INTRUDED
YOU, A SELF-INFLICTED SHOT
ME, A WIDE-OPEN EXIT WOUND

WHEN LOVE ALL BUT HEALS

I loved the night sky so much
that I allowed you to take a needle and thread
and sew your spirit to me—
thousands of little holes covered my body
as though a painter flicked his brush on a blank canvas.

You said my body would finally resemble constellations
when the moonlight peered through me.

Look at that, you said. *You're so full of light.*

CATCHING UP

Do you experience the nights where the air is too empty?
        Where your body is not a body
        but half of a vessel
        needed to swim?

Do you experience the way loneliness
        slips its tongue
        into your mouth
        ever so gently?

Do you give in to it?
        Sigh into
        its mouth?

I'm so sorry that
my lips don't know
how to breathe alone
some nights—

        some nights I am
        less of a person
        and more of the air,
        heavy and vulnerable,
        filling your lungs.

MY BODY IS ANYTHING BUT MINE

my body is anything but mine / it was ripped from me / rests in
the claws of a country / they tell me my body is not a body / but a
habitat for someone else / a man / a child / a thing to be regulated /
my body was taken from me / the night i gave it to a man / who knew
of nothing but hurt / where his hands pooled sorrow / until I was
shrouded in him / and my body was taken from me / when a man
decided it was his / when he was looking to quench his thirst / with
a taste of me / we are wells for them to sip from / fill in / dry out / i
am tired of living in a world / where i belong deeply to anyone / but
myself

HOW TO LOSE YOURSELF

I have studied absence like a theory.

It is all I know how to do:
carry the bodies of those
who abandoned me
as if they are roses
I plan to give to the next
him.

I begin to resemble
every hollow promise,
every fear that has
blossomed into a truth,
until my face contorts
into the nightmares
that embroider my thoughts.

I used to be so pretty
until I lost myself
deep within your absence.

SAYING GOODBYE

i keep stuttering over you / i can't fit you on my tongue anymore / the memories have settled in my mouth / which is to say / i don't know how to speak to you now / i keep stammering over our first kiss / you stumble out of me like knocked-out teeth / piece by piece / it hurts just as bad every time / i guess this is me saying goodbye / i just can't seem to get / the words out

i must give the wounds a new life
rebirth them   call them each by
a new name   a new verse
in order to keep you alive in my words

you are dead to me in every sense but poetry
because i must rewrite your name again
and again so i can remember that your
touch is not a touch but a bullet wound
that my love was not a love but a
lesson for them to hear so they learn
to run at the first warning sign

i will live in the home of my body
and start a house fire if it means
that the ashes will spell out my poems
for all to hear

—*i am still writing about you*

A THANK-YOU NOTE TO MY KILLER

Dearly beloved,

      Thank you for teaching me how to grow skin.

      You think you have peeled away my resilience—left me
a bare, vulnerable thing.

      You did not skin me. You shed a layer of me that
needed to be gone.

      Thank you for showing me what I did not deserve.

      Now I have found all the pieces of the prayer you have
skipped, the words that would summon God.

      Thank you for creating a stronger version of the thing you
thought you killed.

      Thank you for burying me so I could dig myself up with new
hands.

      My love,

      you think you destroyed me.

      The best revenge is letting you know, you did not destroy me,
but instead, restored me.

ON GRIEVING

I often pocket grief
and it beckons me like a lover.
We are so familiar with each other
that grieving no longer becomes
a practice,
a ritual.
I don't need to decorate headstones
to grieve when I do
it for the living all the time.

"WHAT IS GRIEF, IF NOT LOVE PERSEVERING?"
—WandaVision

if not a thread of a promise hanging on a soul?
what is grief, if not the way i return
to a lonely midwest home,
all because i never quite learned how to settle
into the bones of a body, and
sometimes all i know how to do is return to the dead
to ask for tips on living.
i think i've become so intimate with sorrow
that I look for it in every potential lover,
only to find comfort in a brief recognition.
all this to say i think grief is a little more than a persevering love;
it is also a haunting's last stand—
a ghost lingering like a newly forgotten lover.
if i can't shake the grief, maybe i can learn to love it.

HOW DOES ONE BURY A KILLER?

Do I kiss your
forehead, thank
you for the time spent
sparing me?

Do I set you on
fire, tell you this
is how you loved me?

How do I mourn
the loss of
what broke me?

I no longer
know how to
eulogize those who
are still living
in my body—
my body,
a dead thing.

THIS IS HOW THE LIGHT GETS IN

I know I shouldn't thank you
for inhabiting my body —
my body, a broken thing,
a shell of a thing,
a hollow thing that you
slipped your limbs into,
wearing me like a suit.

I know I shouldn't thank you
for painting me with fractures,
skin like fine china, a delicate
thing adorned with beauty,
so easy to break.

I know I shouldn't thank you
for breaking me, but
this is how the light gets in —
broken things turned into windows,
shining carefully through curated cracks.

i've learned how to sew stitches with silk.
to say, this is not broken, nor beautiful,
but a mixture of both. to learn how to break
and repair break and repair,
that there is no ending without a birth.

— *on learning to become*

LEARNING TO BE WHOLE

healing is not
completion of a puzzle
all at once.

here, a piece of a
spine, standing straighter.

here, a piece of a voice
finally returning home
to its throat.

healing happens
piece
by
piece,

recreating yourself.

WHAT IT MEANS TO BE EARTH

Recently, I've learned what it means to be the earth. What I mean is, she has learned so much from dying only to be born again. Time after time, everything she has taken in has betrayed her, tried to end her. Yet all she does is perpetually bloom. I have learned what it means to be the soil you tread on. I have learned what it means to be the life that grows within it. I have learned what it means to be sky, to overlook and be ever-changing. I have learned what it means to be a home to those who forget to be thankful. Let me teach you how to be life, how to have the earth drained from your veins and remind everyone—the universe has spent lifetimes trying to destroy me, but here I am. I am resilient, ethereal. You cannot take what was never yours to begin with.

OPEN LETTER TO AMERICA

America, land of the
free me from these chains bound around my wrist,
these chains you gifted me along with a broken promise
America, the beautiful lies you shoot into the sky
falling like fireworks on the ears of the innocent
America, land of the free to be a citizen when
you do not look like me, free to hold our
bones between your teeth—America, you keep
the lives of children in your mouth yet all you do
is swallow and swallow all of us whole, America
one nation under the God you armed and shackled,
perpetually pulling a trigger, bullets like falling stars
creating holes in bodies you hold up against the light,
call these exit wounds stars and stripes—America, a ghost of
a shipyard you don't even recognize, a grave of oceans that
welcome my ancestors more than you ever will,
an allegiance you pledged to the shadows cast by a
flag waving goodbye—America whose rockets' red
glare and bombs bursting in air fell upon deaf ears on its own land,
America—with liberty and justice for all those who make it out alive.

ALLOW ME TO INTRODUCE MYSELF,

Here I am,
a mosaic of becomings.
I am not entirely
one thing—one person—
but a collection of all
the times I have died,
only to be reborn again
into something different.

Am I a reincarnation,
then? No, I am the
flowers that grow on
a grave, the life that
cultivates the death
and decay to bring out
the beauty from within it.

Feel the raindrops
on your eyelashes
and the sun that
warms them away
—I am both.

I have lived too many
lives to be only one thing,
and instead of attempting
to mesh them into the form
of a human being, I have
decided to love every jagged
edge of mine.

Allow me to introduce myself,

a warning and a welcoming,
all at once.

AN ODE TO NEW BEGINNINGS

My mother gives birth to
my brokenness the way land
gives birth to war—
my body, an aftermath,
curling into her the way
borderlands seek something
to connect to.

Across the world,
in my homeland,
dirt roads and barren
rooftops carry the memories
of a childhood—
innocence and happiness
scattered amidst the dust.

This is what I want to become.

Something beautiful amidst
the broken, a home
amidst the foreign.

My mother carries
bodies inside her,
a bridge between two
worlds, different lifetimes
of poetry settling
in her stomach, ready
to give birth to a new land.

I want to carry her spirit
in me, to remember that
to be a woman is to be a bridge,
and to be alive is to cross
into new possibilities.

ACKNOWLEDGEMENTS

Thank you to Michelle for believing in me and my work, and to Jessica for helping me bring it to life.

Thank you to my family for teaching me what unconditional love is.

Thank you to everyone in the poetry community on Instagram for giving my work such a lovely home and community to be a part of.

And last but certainly not least, thank you to Felix, the love of my life.

Hinnah Mian is a Pakistani American poet and author who placed first in the Emerging Writers Poetry category of the WV Writers Annual Writing Contest in 2020. Her work has appeared in *Kingdoms of the Wild, Harness Magazine, JUMP, Blue Minaret,* and *The Rising Phoenix Review.* Her first book, *To Build a Home,* won silver in the Readers' Favorite International Book Awards.

She spends her time journaling, exploring, and living out her days with the love of her life—her dog, Felix.